40 SCRIPTURE BASED PRAYERS TO PRAY OVER YOUR CHILDREN

KAYLENE YODER

HUMBLE
WISE
PRESS

ISBN: 978-0-9996380-4-0 (print), 978-0-9996380-5-7 (epub)

Publishing and Design Services | MartinPublishingServices.com

Stock Photography: 123rf.com
Contributors: alga38, anamomarques, anskuw, azalia, belchonock, chris_elwell, egal, erostunova, karandaev, kellyplz, kuzmichstudio, loonara, lyulka12, mashe, neirfy, pat138241, photoauris, photoncatcher, prakobkit, saddako, serazetdinov, sinseeho, stephaniefrey, steve_byland, szefei, Taiga, teerawit, tepikina, tomnamon, tuvi, valery_potapova, varts, vladir09, wollertz, yasonya,

CONTENTS

Contents

DEDICATION

For my children,
Cheyenne, Lori, and Ervin

You are my favorites;
you'll always be.
I love you most,
my blessings three.

INTRODUCTION

Parenting remains the one most challenging, yet meaningful role in my life. I'm among the mothers who have hidden in the bathroom to breathe and eat chocolate. I've screamed in my pillow and sobbed large puddles of tears onto the couch.

I've yelled and apologized for it, laughed when I probably shouldn't have, and opted to hold a disobedient child in silence rather than administer a punishment. They knew they did wrong, but at that moment I knew they needed the kindness that leads to repentance, not a punishment that could lead to condemnation.

Seldom can I catch my breath from one situation when another has already begun. Occasionally, my parenting failures make me think it would be appropriate to line up my children and let them take turns at giving me some good old-fashioned, over-the-knee discipline. That would be easier than living with these feelings of inadequacy and the fear of royally messing them up.

I rarely have cut and dried answers when it comes to raising up children. However, I've decided there are two things that are appropriate for every season of parenting – lots of love and lots of prayer.

A wise friend once said, "It's my job to love my children, it's God's job to change them." She was speaking of her adult children, but I think it applies to all ages. So, in my simple way, I choose to lift my children to the Lord and love them where they are at. Even those can be a struggle because I'm either having a hard time liking where they are at, or I'm having a hard time waiting on God to work in their hearts.

However, love and prayer are the only two things I can see being effective for maintaining healthy connected relationships with all my children. After all, I'm not after their perfection as much as I am their hearts. Capture their hearts and they will know how to love. Pray for them and they will be anointed with wisdom, peace, and salvation.

So, my friend, I pray the prayers in this book will help you intercede for your children with all power and authority against the evil one. May you become ever more grounded and strengthened as you steer your children into ways that are right and good. And above all, may you find great peace in knowing that placing your children at the feet of the perfect Father is the safest, most loving place you can put them.

I'm in it with you. Love much and pray big!

Psalm 127:3-5

Children are a heritage from the Lord, offspring a reward from him. Like arrows in the hands of a warrior are children born in one's youth. Blessed is the man whose quiver is full of them.

A PRAYER
FOR MOTHERS

Arise, cry out in the night,
as the watches of
the night begin;
pour out your heart
like water in the
presence of the Lord.
Lift up your hands to Him
for the lives of your children.

Lamentations 2:19

Proverbs 31:26, 28
Titus 2:4-5
Isaiah 40:11

Father, I thank You for this calling of motherhood. Give me a heart of compassion and understanding toward my children. Help me see them as You do; precious souls entrusted to my care for a short time.

Father, I confess the times I have not been an exemplary role model for my children. Search my heart and remove any impatience, harshness, indifference, anger or frustration from me. In those places restore understanding, gentleness, kindness, acceptance, and unconditional love.

Guard my tongue, Lord. Make me one who speaks with wisdom and faithful instruction (Proverbs 31:26), not misleading or harming my children in any way. May my daughter witness me being an example worthy to fashion her own life after, and my son find a standard worth meeting when finding a wife of his own. Lead me into becoming the kind of mother my children may call blessed (Proverbs 31:28).

Father, I pour out my heart in Your presence. "Search me, O God, and know my heart, test me and know my anxious thoughts. See if there is any offensive way in me, and lead me in the way everlasting" (Psalm 139:23-24). Guide me along a path that will build a loving relationship with each child, as well as leave a solid role model for them to follow. In Jesus' name, Amen.

A PRAYER
FOR FATHERS

For you know that
we dealt with each of you
as a father deals
with his own children,
encouraging, comforting,
and urging you to live
lives worthy of God,
who calls you into
His kingdom and glory.

1 Thessalonians 2:11-12

1 Kings 2:2-3
Psalm 78:2-4
Proverbs 13:22
Proverbs 20:7
Ephesians 6:4

Dear Heavenly Father, I lift my children's father to You. Make him a man worthy of this high calling to fatherhood. Gently lead him in the ways of integrity and righteousness, so that his children may see him as an example worth following. Do not let him exasperate his children. Instead, remind him often that they are looking to him for guidance and instruction (Ephesians 6:4).

Where any harm has been done or any rift has occurred in any relationship with his children, Father, give him the courage and humility to reconcile and build up that relationship. Let him not see his children as a hindrance to his plans or his days. Rather, let him see them as blessings and treasures given to him on loan.

Father, I pray my children will be left with a rich spiritual inheritance by the man they call "Dad". Help him be perceptive in his observances of what You require, then may he have the courage to carry out Your call upon his life. May he walk in Your ways and keep Your decrees and commands so that he may prosper in all he does and wherever he goes (1 Kings 2:2-3), giving glory to You for all his children to see.

Teach him how to deal with his own children in the ways You deal with him - gently and lovingly, never in a forceful or demanding manner. Give him patience and wisdom as he guides his children with all encouragement and comfort, urging them to live lives worthy of Your kingdom and Your glory. In Jesus' name, Amen.

3

A PRAYER FOR YOUR CHILD'S WISDOM

Lord, I pray you
would generously supply
my children with wisdom,
and give them the courage
to do what is right.

Amen.

Psalm 111:10
Proverbs 3:7-8
Proverbs 19:20
1 Kings 3:9
2 Timothy 3:14-15

Dear heavenly Father, thank you for children who are teachable in spirit. I pray You would continue nurturing their hearts and minds to be receptive to Your Word; anointing them with wisdom and great insight so that they may discern between right and wrong (1 Kings 3:9).

Father, even a child is known by his actions, whether his deeds are pure and right (Proverbs 20:11). I pray You would grow my children to be known as those who are gentle and kind, seeking Your kingdom first even in the small things. Where they lack discernment, I pray You would generously supply it to them, then add to them the courage to do what is right. Guide their hearts and minds into all that is truth and light.

Lord, Your Word reminds us that wisdom is a shelter to those who have it (Ecclesiastes 7:12). Place in my children a desire to pursue wisdom that can only come from above. Do not let them be wise in their own eyes, but grow to fear You and shun evil more and more each day (Proverbs 3:7-8). Give them a hunger for wisdom and understanding. Plant deep in their hearts a love for You and Your ways, so that they will always turn to You in everything they do and say. In Jesus' name, Amen.

A PRAYER FOR YOUR CHILD'S INTEGRITY

May integrity and uprightness protect me, because my hope is in You.

Psalm 25:21

Psalm 26:2-3
Psalm 139:23-24
Proverbs 10:19
Hebrews 10:22

Father, I lift my children to You asking that You examine their hearts. Grow them to love integrity and walk the way of it. See if there is any offensive way in my children and lead them along the paths of Your everlasting way (Psalm 139:23-24).

Father, I pray that You would reveal to my children any wrong doing or dishonesty in their lives. Then supply them the courage to repent early and have their hearts cleansed from any impurity.

Keep their lips from speaking any vanity or untruth, Lord. Guard them from the temptations to hide from sin or try to cover it with lies. Rather, move them to seek a clear conscience before You. May only what is true, right, and up-building come from my children. Root integrity deep within them, Lord, so they may live protected by truth and confident in their uprightness before You. In Jesus' name, Amen.

A PRAYER FOR YOUR CHILD'S COURAGE

Lord, mark my children as those who are unafraid and unashamed to do what is pleasing in Your sight.

Amen.

1 Chronicles 28:20
Psalm 27:14
2 Timothy 1:7-8

Father, give my children a heart of courage. When they are afraid make Yourself known to them and remind them that You will never leave them nor forsake them.

Help them be strong and courageous to do the good work You would have them do. Make them capable of doing great things, yet satisfied in the mundane routines of everyday life. Give my children a desire to do what is right, Father. Give them the courage to walk in Your ways and do as You require, so that it may go well with them and that they may prosper in all they do (1 Kings 2:2-3).

Mark my children as those who are unafraid and unashamed to do what is pleasing in Your sight. Lord, You have not given them a spirit of fear and timidity, but one of power, love and self-discipline (2 Timothy 1:7-8). May they stand brave in the face of what is before them, shining the light of Your love and grace everywhere they go and to whomever they meet. In Jesus' name, Amen.

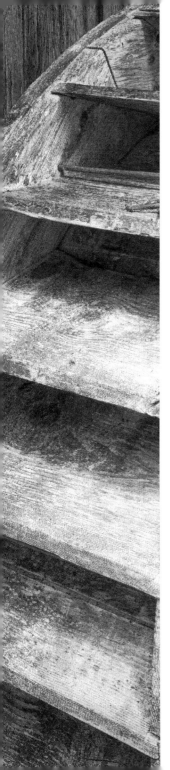

6

A PRAYER FOR YOUR CHILD'S HUMILITY

Humility and the fear of the Lord bring wealth and honor and life.

Proverbs 22:4

Romans 12:3
Philippians 2:3-4
James 3:13
James 4:10

Dear Jesus, thank You for setting the bar as the ultimate life of humility. You have taught us that we should not think of ourselves more highly than we ought, but to think of ourselves with sober judgment (Romans 12:3). I pray this for my children; help them to honor others above themselves, even when it's difficult or circumstances seem unfair. Establish them so firmly in Your Word that they have no desire to seek glorification from others, or take justification in their own hands. Help them live in ways that will gain them Your praise, favor, and protection.

Father, You tell us that You bless a humble person with wealth, honor, life, and wisdom (Proverbs 11:2, 22:4). So develop in my children a heart that is gentle and compliant to Your will, always ready to do what is good. Help them stay away from slandering others, and instead promote love and peace, being considerate in all things, demonstrating humility toward all (Titus 3:1-2).

Lord, teach my children that a humble person walks securely, and that You will vindicate, reward, and uphold all who live according to Your Word. Teach my children to be still and quiet in their souls, placing their hope and trust solidly on Your foundation. May they have no desire to build or claim a kingdom of their own. May they boast only of You and what is Yours. In Jesus' name, Amen.

A PRAYER FOR YOUR CHILD'S OBEDIENCE

Father, give my
children a desire to
love You, serve you,
and obey You
in all they do.

Amen.

Deuteronomy 13:3-4
Job 36:11-12
John 14:23
James 1:25
2 John 6

Father, I pray You would incline my children's hearts toward obedience. Give them a desire to love You and want to serve You, following Your will in everything they do.

Father, Your Word encourages us to be obedient and respectful to authority. Give my children hearts that are willing to obey their parents, teachers, mentors, law enforcement, governments, and the like, while still upholding Your Word as supreme authority in their lives.

Father, I pray You would guide honorable influences into my children's lives, giving them solid examples of right standing to fashion their lives after. Give my children wisdom in knowing when someone or something may be misleading them. Help them look intently into Your perfect law so they may not be misguided by other people. Make them recipients of Your warnings and courageous followers of Your nudges. After they have proven obedience, Father, I pray You would bless them in mighty ways. May they spend their days in prosperity and their years in contentment (Job 36:11-12).

Again, Lord, I pray that You would impress upon my children a heart for obedience. Test them to find out whether they love You with all their hearts and souls. Help them understand that it is You they must follow and revere. And help them walk boldly in Your commands, serving You and holding fast to You (Deuteronomy 13:3-4), so they may experience the blessings You have for them. Withhold no good thing from them for the honorable ways they conduct their lives. In Jesus' name, Amen.

8

A PRAYER FOR YOUR CHILD'S HEART

Father, I pray You would give my child a heart that is soft and pliable to Your will and Your ways.

Amen.

Psalm 51:10
Psalm 86:11-12
Luke 6:45
Acts 15:9

Father, I pray You would impress Yourself upon the hearts of my children. Help them understand how the breadth, depth, and height of Your love includes them intimately. Do not let their hearts flounder or wander in any insecurity or uncertainty of Your love.

Father, I also pray that you would search their hearts for anything that does not glorify You. Where there is any bitterness, anger, wrong motivations, harmful intentions or the like, I pray You would bring conviction and then remove it from them. Soften their hearts and place in them a new heart and a steadfast spirit (Psalm 51:10). Keep purifying their hearts by their faith (Acts 15:9), examining them and leading them in Your everlasting way (Psalm 139:23-24).

Father, I pray You would make them teachable, loving, pure, and without fault. Reward them according to their conduct. May they live from a heart that is a wellspring of good, blessing the lives of all those around them. Teach them to love the things You love and continually seek You in all they do, so their hearts may be proven pure and right before God and men. In Jesus' name, Amen.

A PRAYER FOR YOUR CHILD'S MIND

Lord, open my children's
minds that they
may understand the
Scriptures more and more.

Amen.

(Luke 24:45)

Romans 8:5-6
Romans 12:2
Philippians 4:8-9
1 Peter 1:13

Father, I pray You would protect and guide my children's minds. Direct their thoughts in ways that are pleasing to You, Lord. Do not let them be given over to the sinful desires of human nature or the dangerous wanderings of the mind. Make them capable of weighing, understanding, and acting on truth. Do not let their minds go uncorrected to the point that they would cause pain to others or themselves.

Father, keep my children from thought processes that lead to anxiety, depression, self pity, pride, adultery, deception, or any kind of impurity. Help them think only on things that are true and praiseworthy. Remind them to dwell on facts and not be directed solely by how they feel. Guide them into all purity and sound thought processes.

Father, I pray You would guard their hearts and their minds in Christ Jesus (Philippians 4:7). Let them be transformed by the daily renewal of their minds, training themselves to focus on what is Your good and perfect will (Romans 12:2).

As they grow up into Your likeness, Father, I pray You would open their minds like a gate and let Your wisdom and understanding flow in, maturing and nurturing them to a greater love for You and increased knowledge of Your Holy Word (Luke 24:45). In Jesus' name, Amen.

10

A PRAYER FOR THE PATHS YOUR CHILD WALKS

Father, set my children's hearts upon You, so they may know the paths You have called them to.

Amen.

Psalm 1:1
Proverbs 4:25-27
Proverbs 5:21
Jeremiah 6:16

Father, I pray You would preserve my children's paths. Go before them and prepare the way with wisdom and integrity, making the way smooth for them to walk in.

Father, when they are faced with choices, I pray they would consult You and other wise counsel before they make any decisions. Anoint them with great insight in choosing the way they should walk and behave. Remind them that Your way is good and right and that You require honesty, humility and mercy (Micah 6:8).

Father, we know that all our ways are in full view of You and that You examine all our paths (Proverbs 5:21). I pray my children will keep their eyes fixed upon You, pursuing heavenly goals and not swerving onto paths that are not good. May they walk in love, always in right standing with You, Father.

Continue giving them a knowledge of good and evil. Keep their feet from walking in ways that could harm themselves or others. Whatever they do and wherever they go, may they go with great confidence and peace that comes when You say, "This is the way; walk in it" (Isaiah 30:21). In Jesus' name, Amen.

11

A PRAYER FOR YOUR CHILD'S REPENTANCE AND SALVATION

Father, draw my
children to Yourself with
Your kindness, so they may
come to know You
intimately as their
Heavenly Father.

Amen.

Psalm 103:8-13
Proverbs 28:13
Isaiah 43:25
Romans 10:9-11
1 John 1:9-10

Father, I thank you for giving my children hearts that can be taught and made pliable to Your Word. I pray You would develop in them a desire to do Your will and seek Your ways in all they do. Do not let them become contaminated by any sin that is rooted in pride or self glorifying ways. Help them live transparent and pure before You, confessing and renouncing sin as You reveal it so they may find mercy and favor in Your sight.

Father, if there is any sin in my children, hidden or apparent, I pray You would gently convict them of it. Allow them an appropriate sorrow over any sin, then give them the courage and ability to repent of it. Lift up their chins with the hope and knowledge of redemption. Be quick to assure them of Your love and forgiveness, Father. Let them know that You are slow to anger and abounding in love toward them (Nehemiah 9:17). Do not let them become discouraged, but rather more and more thankful and dependent on Your great grace.

Father, I pray You would speak to my children's hearts daily. Draw them to Yourself with Your kindness so they may come to know You at an early age. Increase their desire to love You and serve You as their one and only Master. Nurture my children into an ever-increasing faith, marking them as one of Your children driving hard after Your heart. In Jesus name, Amen.

A PRAYER
FOR THE
WORDS YOUR
CHILD SPEAKS

May the words of
my mouth and the
meditation of my heart
be pleasing in Your sight,
O Lord, my rock
and my redeemer.

Psalm 19:14

Proverbs 15:1-2
Proverbs 20:19
Proverbs 21:23
Colossians 4:6
2 Timothy 2:16

Father, Your Word tells us where there are many words, sin is not absent. I pray You would make my children aware of what they speak. Give them discretion to weigh their thoughts before any words are spoken. Do not let any unwholesome talk come out of their mouths, but only what is helpful to all who hear (Ephesians 4:29). Help them shy away from obscene language, course joking, and foolish talk (Ephesians 5:4). Should they be tempted to indulge in reckless, unchecked words, restrain them with the reminder that the one "who guards his mouth and his tongue keeps himself from calamity (Proverbs 21:23).

Father, along with discretion, I pray You would embolden my children to speak the truth in love even when it is hard. Should they cause any harm by the words they have spoken, supply them the courage and humility to seek reconciliation. Place a guard upon my children's lips, renewing their hearts and minds, so the words of their mouths and the meditations of their hearts may be pleasing to You (Psalm 19:14).

Father, when feelings overwhelm and they don't know what to say or how to express themselves appropriately, strengthen them with Your peace. Calm them and assure them that even though the storm is real, You hear their cries and answer their calls. Furthermore, speak truth to my children about themselves and the situations they are in. If at anytime they think or speak evil or negatively of themselves, help them see themselves as You do; precious and dearly loved, a masterpiece beautiful in Your eyes. In Jesus' name, Amen.

A PRAYER FOR YOUR CHILD'S ATTITUDE

Lord, do not let my children be overcome with anger, bitterness, regret, pride, or selfishness. Rather, give them an attitude like Christ's, humble and willing to serve others.

Amen.

Romans 12:10-13
Philippians 2:5-8
Ezekiel 36:26-27

Jesus, thank you for giving us a perfect example of an attitude that is pleasing to the Lord. I pray You would help my children fashion their demeanor and temperament after Yours; humble, gentle, caring, deferring, and confident.

Father, when life is hard or seems unfair, do not let my children be overcome with attitudes of anger, bitterness, regret, pride, or selfishness. Instead, give them wisdom and strength to not conform to the patterns and mindsets of the world. Give each of my children a desire to pursue a new heart and a new spirit. Convict them in any areas where they may need to rid themselves of world inspired attitudes and refill them with hearts of gentleness. Father, put Your Spirit within my children and move them to follow Your will and Your ways (Ezekiel 36:26-27).

Lord, help my children honor others above themselves, to seek a heart after Yours, to radiate the joy of hope, and maintain an attitude of patience in the trenches of life. May they be known for their genuine love and care for all those around them (Romans 12:10-13). In Jesus' name, Amen.

A PRAYER FOR YOUR CHILD'S CHARACTER

Lord, I pray You would establish my children's characters in the knowledge of good and evil according to Your Word.

Amen.

1 Thessalonians 5:21-22

Proverbs 6:16-19
Proverbs 22:1
Galatians 5:22-26
1 Thessalonians 5:21-22

Father God, thank You for giving my children a knowledge of good and evil. I pray that by Your mercy You would lead them into Your presence where they may come to know You more fully. Through Your goodness, entice them to become more like You in all they say and do. May the fruit they bear leave behind an aroma that magnifies Your name.

Father, I pray You would build each of my children's characters in humility and transparency. Do not let them make hasty decisions that could harm others or themselves. Keep them honest and self-controlled in all their daily dealings. Remind them to be wise and upright at all times, testing everything, holding on to the good, and avoiding every kind of evil (1 Thessalonians 5:21-22). Through their good character, Lord, help my children establish respectable and honorable names. May they always hold to ways that are most honoring to You. In Jesus' name, Amen.

15

A PRAYER FOR YOUR CHILD'S LOVE FOR OTHERS

Lord, teach my children how great Your love is for them, so that they may become those who carry Your affection to all those they meet.

Amen.

Romans 8:38-39
Romans 12:9-10
Ephesians 5:1-2
1 Corinthians 13:1-8

Father, I praise You for sending Your Son and giving us the perfect example of love. You have shown us how to love others the way they need to be loved and not how they deserve to be loved. I pray You will put such an unselfish love in my childrens' hearts.

Father, do not let my children do anything out of selfish ambition or vain conceit. Instead, in humility, let them consider others better than themselves (Philippians 2:3-4). Teach them not to seek their own ways, or have ulterior motives when they serve others. Help them be genuinely concerned about other people's physical and spiritual well-being. Teach them that love is patient and kind, not envious, boastful, proud, rude, or easily angered (1 Corinthians 13:4-8). Help them lay down their agendas and plans when it is edifying to others to do so. Teach them to give themselves up for others, but not be taken advantage of in harmful ways. Help them give more than they take, so that through their gentle, servant-minded love they may receive a lasting reward.

Father, I pray my children will learn to love You more and more each day. Remind them often that neither life nor death, neither angels nor demons, neither the present nor the future, neither height nor depth, nor anything else in all creation, will be able to separate them from Your great love (Romans 8:38-39). May this truth give them an ever increasing desire to walk in obedience to Your command to love You first and then others. In Jesus' precious name, Amen.

16

A PRAYER FOR YOUR CHILD'S JOY

Lord, grant my children eternal blessings and make them glad with the joy of Your presence.

Amen.

(Psalm 21:6)

Psalm 13:5-6
Psalm 16:11
Psalm 30:11
Psalm 94:19
Habakkuk 3:18-19

Dear Heavenly Father, thank You for promising Your strength to us. We find joy in being able to rely on You when trials blaze. I pray that Your consolation during the harder times of life will be a source of joy for my children. Do not let them be distraught and burdened beyond what they can bear, Lord. Let them rest in the knowledge that You bring nothing that will harm or destroy Your faithful ones.

Father, I pray that You would teach my children to see trials for what they are: the testing of their faith. Help them endure Your refining work as an examination of their belief in You. Through the trials, prove to my children that You are their strength and comfort, and will enable them to go the heights (Habakkuk 3:18-19). Father, when my children have remained steadfast in You, complete their joy as they look back and see growth and maturity in themselves (James1:2-4). Make them grateful for trials, even while Your contentment and joy settles into the painful places.

Lord, help my children trust in You no matter what storms or seasons they face. When life is easy for a time, remind them not to take it for granted, but continue to prepare their hearts and minds with Your Word. Lord, should they cross turbulent waters, teach them Your unfailing love so they will not forsake You. Grant them eternal blessings and make them glad with the joy of Your presence (Psalm 21:6). In Jesus' name, Amen.

17

A PRAYER FOR YOUR CHILD'S PEACE

Lord, surround my children with Your peace, so they will not be anxious about anything.

Amen.

Psalm 119:165
Numbers 6:24-26
Isaiah 26:3
Philippians 4:6-7

Dear Heavenly Father, we find great encouragement in the knowledge that You have overcome the world (John 16:33). Thank You that in You we may have peace at all times and in every way (2 Thessalonians 3:16).

Father, when darts of the evil one are being fired at my children, keep them steadfast in Your love. May Your calming hand and Your unwavering presence help them to not be anxious about anything, but in everything turn to You in prayer and petition (Philippians 4:6-7). Impart peace beyond measure upon my children, confirming to them that You are not slack in Your promises. Surround them with Your blessed assurance so they will not succumb to the temptations of despair, hopelessness, depression, or distrust in You.

Father, move my children to be among those who promote peace in all they do. Do not let them be quick to argue or seek revenge, Lord. You have not made my children to be foolish, but to operate in courageous faith. Help them be kind, patient, and loving, making every effort to do what leads to peace and mutual edification of those around them (Romans 14:19).

Father, let my children's hearts overflow with Your peace and spill out of their lives for all to see. I ask that You give them a desire to love You and serve You more and more each day, so that Your peace beyond understanding may become a familiar existence to them. In Jesus' name, Amen.

A PRAYER FOR YOUR CHILD'S PATIENCE

Lord, clothe my children with strength and wisdom, so they may continually persevere in doing what is good.

Amen.

Ephesians 4:2
Colossians 1:9-12
Colossians 3:12-13
1 Thessalonians 5:14-15

Lord, thank You for being such a patient and gracious Father. I praise You for Your mercies that are never ending. Lord, I pray that You would give each of my children a heart like Yours; patient, understanding, and long suffering.

Father, Your Word tells us a person's wisdom gives them great patience and that it is to their glory to overlook an offense (Proverbs 19:11). Lord, I ask that You would anoint my children with the wisdom that will help them choose patience in circumstances that may seem overwhelming or impossible. Do not let them lose heart, but rather persevere in faith so they may reap an eternal reward.

Lord, work in my children's hearts that they may uproot any impatience, grudges, anger, jealous tendencies, or harsh words. In those places, teach them to be completely humble and gentle, bearing with others in love (Ephesians 4:2), forgiving as You do, completely and quickly. Help my children clothe themselves with kindness and compassion (Colossians 3:12-13). May they see that Your way is never wrong, no matter how difficult it may seem.

Lord, fill my children with the knowledge of Your will through all spiritual wisdom and understanding. I trust that by Your powerful grace they will live a life worthy of You. May they please You in every way, Lord, bearing fruit in every good work and growing in the knowledge of You. Strengthen them according to Your glorious might, so that they may have great endurance to run the race marked out before them (Colossians 1:9-11). In Jesus' precious name, Amen.

19

A PRAYER FOR YOUR CHILD'S KINDNESS

Lord, impress Your kindness upon my children, so that they may learn to live with peace of mind, good reputation, and receive eternal rewards.

Amen.

Proverbs 11:17
Luke 6:35
Ephesians 4:31-32
2 Peter 1:5-8

Father, thank You for Your kindness. Your mercies are never ending, reaching even to the ungrateful and wicked. Lord, teach my children to be kind to others, to love their enemies and do good to those who mistreat them (Luke 6:35). Work in their hearts, reminding them to never pay back wrong for wrong, or insult for insult, but to always be kind to all people (1 Thessalonians 5:15).

Father, I pray You would move my children's hearts to rid themselves of any bitterness, rage, anger, brawling, slander, or any other form of malice. Instead, grow my children to have kind and compassionate hearts toward others, forgiving others as You have forgiven them (Ephesians 4:31-32). Also, Father, work sincerity in my children, so that they will not have ulterior motives for being kind, but display a true compassion in all they do and say.

Father, Your Word says a kind person ultimately benefits himself (Proverbs 11:17). I pray that You would greatly reward my children's upright and pure lives. Make them successful in all they do. Bless them with the benefits of long term peace of mind, good reputation, and eternal blessings. In Jesus' name, Amen.

A PRAYER FOR YOUR CHILD'S GOODNESS

Lord, pour out
Your wisdom and
discernment upon my
children so they may
know the way that
is good and godly.

Amen.

Romans 12:9
1 Corinthians 10:23-24
Galatians 6:9-10
1 Peter 2:12

Dear Jesus, thank You for being our good Father, the One who promises to never leave nor forsake. The One who sticks closer than a brother, always encouraging and correcting to our benefit. Lord, I ask that You continue displaying Your goodness toward my children. Thank you for the times You have kept them from making bad choices; the times You intervened to save them from things that could harm them or cause regret.

Father, teach my children to seek You first. Through the constant use of your Word, may they train themselves in the way that is good and godly. When they are at the crossroads of good and evil, Lord, pour out Your wisdom and discernment upon them so they may know the way that is beneficial in Your eyes. Then, pour Your strength and peace upon them, encouraging them to walk in the way of uprightness.

Father, I pray my children will seek the greater good of those around them (1 Corinthians 10:24). May they work toward mutual edification in all situations, so that even pagans can see Your good work through them (1 Peter 2:12). Father, I pray You would impress upon my children to lead disciplined lives, to be clear minded and self-controlled, loving and serving others in Your name. Do not let them grow weary in doing what is right, for at the proper time You promise a harvest if they do not give up (Galatians 6:9-10). In Jesus' name, Amen.

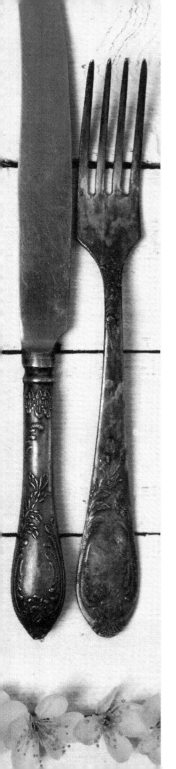

A PRAYER FOR YOUR CHILD'S FAITHFULNESS

Lord, give my children hearts that are faithful to You, so they may find blessing in all they do.

Amen.

Psalm 18:25-36
Psalm 31:23
Psalm 86:15
1 Corinthians 4:2

Jesus, thank You for Your faithfulness, even to the cross. You have proven to be our Rock, our Guide, our compassionate and gracious God, slow to anger, abounding in love and faithfulness (Psalm 86:15).

Lord, I pray You would give my children an urgent desire to grow in Your likeness. Teach them to be those of courageous faith, standing for what is good and right in Your eyes. I pray my children will be on their guard against anything that does not bring life and godliness. Help them discern good from evil, making them wise to the ways of the world and the lord of it, the enemy.

Father, give my children the courage to apply Your standard to their lives so that they may be known as a righteous people. Make them faithful in little so they may become faithful in much (Luke 16:10). Make them pure in thought and deed, always being guided by Your Word so they may claim lives holy and blameless before You. Write Your Word on the tablet of their hearts so their faithfulness to You may become more and more evident each day. In Jesus' name, Amen.

22

A PRAYER
FOR YOUR
CHILD'S
SELF-CONTROL

Father, through Your
great grace, teach
my children to
clothe themselves with
self-control, rejecting
ungodliness and
worldly passions.

Amen.

Proverbs 16:32
1 Peter 5:8-9
Proverbs 29:11
Titus 2:12

Father God, I come before You, thankful for these children You have blessed me with. I pray that You would continue renewing their minds and showing them Your will and Your way. Make my children workmen worthy of what You have called them to do.

Lord, remove any traits that are overbearing, quick tempered, or self advancing. Do not let them be given to drunkenness, violence, filthy language, or pursue dishonest gain. In their hearts, Lord, restore hospitality; make them good, self-controlled, upright, holy, and disciplined. Help them hold firm to Your trustworthy way (Titus 1:7-9).

Lord, we know our enemy, the devil, prowls around like a roaring lion looking for someone to devour (1 Peter 5:8). Today, I stand against his wicked schemes to make my children fall. I proclaim that my children, strong and in the power of Your might, can resist the plans of the evil one. Strengthen and uphold my children making them able to resist the darts of temptation fired at them. Supply them the ability to easily discern right from wrong and give them the power and the ability to say "No" to temptations.

Jesus, You are the perfect example of One who is clear-minded and self-controlled. Teach my children to be the same: temperate, worthy of respect, faithful, loving, and patient, showing integrity in all they do through their seriousness and soundness of speech. Furthermore, may those who oppose my children be ashamed because they can find nothing bad to say about them (Titus 2:8).

Through Your great grace, teach my children to clothe themselves with self-control, rejecting ungodliness and worldly passions. In Jesus' name, Amen.

23

PRAYING THE ARMOR OF GOD OVER YOUR CHILD

Lord, equip my children with all spiritual strength and armor, so they may walk confidently in Your will and Your ways.

Amen.

Ephesians 6:10-18
Ephesians 3:16-21

Father God, thank you for providing us with spiritual armor that we may stand strong against our adversary, the devil. I pray this armor over my children now, so they may become equipped with power, strength, and favor throughout their lives.

Father, give my children a desire to love you and the willingness to serve You. Set their hearts upon You and give them a taste for Your Word. Help them wrap the belt of Your truth tightly around their hearts and minds so they may be able to discern good from evil. Keep Your Word bound close to them, so that they measure all their thoughts according to Your Word. When they speak may they weigh their words according to Your truth.

Lord, give my children a desire to put on Your breastplate of righteousness, living a life that is in right standing with You. May they apply Your standards in all they do and say.

Move my children to strap on the shoes of peace, Father, so they will not be frightened by any situation. May they walk confidently into any place You have called them to knowing that You are with them. Let them gain a clear mind so they do not need to be terrified about anything.

Father, equip my children with the shield of faith. Keep them completely grounded, centered, and protected in whatever they are called to do. Should their faith begin to wear thin, Lord, remind them they only need to cry out to You and You will supply them with more strength and grace. Help them cling tightly to this shield so they will not lose their hope in You.

Next, Lord, remind my children to strap down their helmet of salvation, the divine hardhat that tells the devil exactly who they are – a child of God. Should he dare mess with Your children, we know he ultimately messes with You. Lord, keep my children's identity in You engraved on their hearts, minds, and souls so they will not forget who they are and Whose they are.

Lord, give my children continual exposure and ready

availability to the sword of the Spirit, which is Your Word. Do not let them forget it, disown it, reject it, or abuse it. Every time they turn around make it be right there, reminding them You are always near and speaking. Give my children the desire to be fluent in Your Word, so they may know how to live, how to speak, and how to ward off the enemy with Your truth.

Finally, Lord, let my children come before you in prayer, boldly asking whatever they need in Your name. Loose their tongues, Lord, that they may speak with confidence and expectancy, trusting that what they ask of You, will be done for them.

Lord, I pray all these things will become my children's spiritual wardrobe more and more. Teach them to dress in it daily so they may continually walk in Your power, strength, and blessing. In Jesus name, Amen.

Trust
Scripture Readings

Jeremiah 17:5-8

Isaiah 43:1-4

Isaiah 40:27-31

Isaiah 55:8-13

Psalm 28:6-9

Isaiah 41:8-14

Psalm 13:1-6

Psalm 31:1-8

Psalm 31:14-20

Psalm 118:5-13

24

A PRAYER FOR YOUR CHILD TO TRUST THE LORD

The Lord is good, a refuge in times of trouble. He cares for those who trust in Him.

Nahum 1:7

Psalm 32:10
Proverbs 84:11-12
Isaiah 28:16
Jeremiah 17:7

Father, I thank You for Your steadfast and proven ways. From the beginning of time You have been faithful to carry out Your promises to us.

I pray now that You would grow each of my children in the knowledge of Your trustworthiness. Help them understand that nothing will happen in their life that You don't know about or care deeply about. When the days are hard and hope seems dim, give them an extra dose of trust. Help them dig in their faith heels and hold on to You. Do not let them forget that You are good, a refuge in times of trouble, and that You care about those who trust in You (Nahum 1:7).

Father, Your Word says You count blessed those whose confidence is in You (Jeremiah 17:7). I pray You would enable my children to trust You more and more each day. Prove Yourself to them so they may be convinced beyond a doubt that Your ways are good and right. Then help them walk in righteousness so they may thrive in all they do (Proverbs 11:28). In Jesus' name, Amen.

A PRAYER FOR YOUR CHILD'S HEALTH

Father, protect and reinforce my children's bodies with health and strength.

Amen.

Romans 12:1
1 Corinthians 6:19-20
3 John 1:2

Father, thank you that You have blessed my children with healthy bodies. You have knit them together beautifully and perfectly in Your sight. You know them inside and out, to the most intricate detail. I praise You, Father, for their lives.

Lord, I pray that You would protect and strengthen their bodies against any harmful invasions of diseases, sicknesses, and other health altering situations. Where there may be any weakness or potential vulnerability in their bodies, protect and reinforce them with health and strength.

Father, I pray You would also motivate each of my children to care for their body in a manner that promotes health and is well-pleasing to You. Help them know that our bodies are the temples where Your Spirit resides and meets with us personally; a sacred place where You come to dwell (1 Corinthians 3:16-17). Remove any tendencies toward laziness or indifference in caring for themselves and replace it with an awareness that what they put in their vessel has the ability to harm or nourish their body. So whether it is regular bathing, making better food choices, exercising, eliminating addictions, or any other way to appropriately care for their body, Father, help my children make wise choices.

Father, Your Word also says that to bring health to our body and nourishment to our bones, we must fear You and shun evil (Proverbs 3:7-8). I pray fervently, Lord, that You would impress Yourself upon my children and give them an appropriate awe of You. Give them the ability to recognize evil and supply them the strength to shun it so they may flourish in abundant health of mind, body, and soul. In Jesus' mighty name, Amen.

A PRAYER FOR YOUR CHILD'S PROTECTION

Father, I deposit my children back into Your hands, trusting that You will watch over them both now and forevermore.

Amen.

Psalm 5:11-12
Psalm 32:6-8
Psalm 91:9-12
Psalm 121:7-8
Psalm 139:3-5
Proverbs 18:10

Father, I thank You that You invite us into Your protection; that when we seek You and make You our God that You promise to command Your angels to watch over us (Psalm 91:9-12).

I pray now that You would protect my children as they go throughout their days. Hem them in, behind and before, and lay Your hand upon them (Psalm 139:5). Do not let any harm come to them. Keep each of my children safe beneath Your wings and guard them against any plots that are meant to harm or bring ruin to them. Be close to each of my children, Father, surround them with Your favor as with a shield (Psalm 5:11-12).

I pray You would protect them in all the ways they walk; in their coming out and their going in. Guard them against diseases of the mind and body, accidents, predators, and all kinds of evil and evil-doers. Anoint each of my children with Your favor and protection, letting them rest safely between Your shoulders (Deuteronomy 33:12).

Father, as my children walk through their days, I pray You would give them clear direction in doing Your will, so they may remain within the safety of Your cover. Give them wisdom to know when to shy away from potential harm, both physically and spiritually. Then help them courageously walk away from it. May the blood of Jesus wash over each of my children, protecting them as they walk through this day and every day of their lives. In Jesus' mighty name, Amen.

A PRAYER FOR YOUR CHILD'S CHOICES

Lord, help my children choose life over death and blessings over curses, so they may live long lives in Your favor.

Amen.

Deuteronomy 30:19-20
Proverbs 8:10-11
Proverbs 19:20-21
Ephesians 5:15-16

Father, thank You for giving my children sound minds that are capable of making wise choices. Guide them to make decisions based on Your Word. I pray they would not act or speak in ways they may later regret. Help them refrain from ways that could cause others to question their motives or character.

Father, I pray my children would remain humble and teachable in heart, choosing Your instruction over the ways of the world, seeking wisdom rather than riches. May they listen to advice and sound teaching so they may steer clear of harmful situations.

Lord, interrupt any enticement my children may have to go a shorter, self-advancing route in life. Instead, give them insight to know the better way, followed by the integrity to go it. When life is hard and the road seems dark, remind my children to choose to trust You in the unknown. Help them remain steadfast, using Your Word as their lighthouse, a beacon of hope guiding them through the storms of life.

Father, You have set before us life and death, blessings and curses (Deuteronomy 30:19-20). May my children always choose life, so they may walk blessed before You. May they always be careful how they live – not as unwise but as wise, making the most of every opportunity (Ephesians 5:15-16). May the choices they make be consistent with Your Word and character. In Jesus' name, Amen.

A PRAYER FOR YOUR CHILD'S EXAMPLE

Lord, help my children be imitators of Jesus, living unashamed and blameless before You.

Amen.

1 Peter 2:19-21
1 Timothy 4:12
2 Timothy 2:15, 22-24
Titus 1:7

Father, thank You for sending Your Son, the perfect example for us to fashion our lives after. I pray that my children would find great value and purpose in living a life that brings honor and glory to You.

Father, even children are known by their conduct. Help my children be imitators of Jesus, living unashamed and blameless before You. Guide my children to pursue righteousness, faith, love, and peace (2 Timothy 2:22), so that their ways may be a good example to those around them even though they are young (1 Timothy 4:12).

Father, when my children are in hard situations give them the courage to do the right thing. Strengthen them to stand for what is correct in Your eyes even when it may not be popular or the easy thing to do. Make my children bold and wise, always choosing to shine their lights for what is good and upstanding. Make them leaders in honoring You, so others may be encouraged to walk uprightly as well.

I lift my children to You, Father, asking that You guide them in the ways they should go. May they do their best to present themselves as those approved, as workmen who do not need to be ashamed, and who handle the Word of God correctly (2 Timothy 2:15). May the example of their lives be as those who willingly walk in the ways You lead. In Jesus' name, Amen.

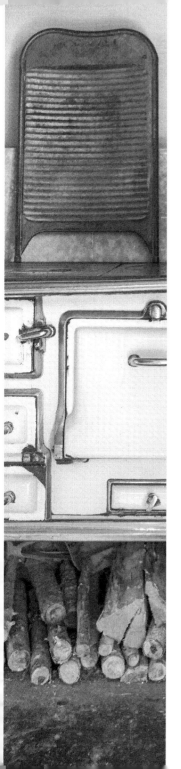

29

A PRAYER FOR YOUR CHILD'S FRIENDS

Lord, I ask that You would lead godly friends and influences into each of my children's lives.

Amen.

Proverbs 13:20
Proverbs 16:28-29
Proverbs 22:24-25
1 Corinthians 15:33

Lord, I lift my children to You in regard to their friendships. You have not put them on this earth with the intent for them to walk in solitude, so as iron sharpens iron, I pray You would lead godly friends and influences into each of my children's lives.

Father, I know it is hard to find friends who are trustworthy, but I pray You would lead my children to people who will build them up and encourage their faith. When it seems all the world is against them, remind my children that You are the one friend who sticks closer than a brother (Proverbs 18:24). When the road looks dark before them, make them aware of Your presence; that You never leave nor forsake. May they seek You always in filling the voids that an earthly being should never fill.

Father, we know bad company corrupts good character (1 Corinthians 15:33), and far too often misleads the unsuspecting. Make my children aware and capable of recognizing when they may need to remove, distance, or guard themselves from a person or relationship. Give them no interest in pursuing friendships that could harm their life, reputation, or faith.

Lord, I pray also that You would teach my children how to be a friend to those who need a little encouragement. Help my children behave in ways that would attract godly friends, so both parties may be helped in their walk with You. Nudge my children to be patient, caring, gentle, and courageous in being a positive influence in another's life, while still making wise choices in their friendships. In Jesus' name, Amen.

A PRAYER FOR STRONG SIBLING RELATIONSHIPS

Father, work in my children to be patient and kind to each other, protecting the bond of unity among them.

Amen.

Psalm 133
Romans 12:9-10
Romans 15:5
1 Peter 3:8-9

Father God, thank You for each of my children. I pray that You would give them a desire to protect the bond of unity among themselves (Romans 15:5). Help them be devoted to each other in brotherly love and honor one another above themselves (Romans 12:9-10).

Lord, inspire my children to work together for the good of each other, living and growing in harmony each day. Help them be compassionate and humble in the way they do life together. When differences arise, spur them toward reconciliation so the friction may be dissolved quickly and in ways that benefit both parties. Help them be self-controlled and wise in their words and actions toward each other. Lord, where there is unity You bestow blessings and life (Psalm 133). I pray this would be so for my children's relationships throughout their whole lives.

Father, teach my children how to be patient and kind to each other. Do not let envy or pride take root in their hearts. Keep them from dealing rudely or angrily with each other. Help them forgive wholly and completely, not letting grudges or bitterness sour their hearts against each other. Lord, help my children protect their family ties, trust each other, hope for the best for each other, and persevere in building each other up in love and truth. In Jesus' name, Amen.

A PRAYER FOR YOUR CHILD'S LIFE PARTNER

Father, guide each of my children to the spouse perfectly designed for them; the one they may live with, laugh with, and love all the days of their life.

Amen.

Mark 10:6-9
1 Corinthians 7:1-7
1 Corinthians 10:13
Hebrews 13:4-5

Father God, I lift my children to You asking that You maneuver and steer them in paths pleasing to You. Along those paths, I pray You would reveal to them Your plan for their life regarding marriage or singleness.

If it is singleness, Lord I pray You would surround them with Your love and assurance that Your plan for them is beautiful and full of purpose. Be their Rock and steady hand, guiding them to places and things that will bring meaning and fulfillment to their lives. In singleness, help them remain pure, not swayed or weakened by the enemy's plans to defile.

Father, if Your design for my children holds marriage, I pray You would lead them to the life partner who will build them up in ways that bring glory and honor to You. I pray You would keep both my child and their significant other pure in heart, mind, and body. Do not let either of them be swayed by sexual immorality, pornography, homosexuality, or transgender-ism. I pray they would see their bodies as holy and sacred ground, not defiling each other or themselves. Keep their desires pure, their hands clean, and their hearts without evil intent.

Father, place a desire in my children and their spouses to love You more than they love each other. In this way they will be able to love each other with a pure love; one that is humble, whole, and transparent. May each of them expect You to be the One who fills all their expectations, so they may be kept strong during disappointments or temptations to seek affection outside of their marriage covenant. Keep their hearts true to one another, lest they be enticed into one of the enemy's tunnels of sin.

Father, I pray each of my children and their spouse would come to know You at a young age and continue growing in grace, forgiveness, servant-hood, and integrity throughout their lives. Whatever the path's of their lives may hold, keep them centered on You so they may know the gift of marriage in richness and joy. In Jesus' name, Amen.

A PRAYER FOR YOUR CHILD TO LEAD A PURE LIFE

Father, guard my children with purity of heart, mind, soul, and body.

Amen.

Psalm 24:3-4
1 Thessalonians 4:3-7
James 4:7-8
2 Peter 3:14

Dear Heavenly Father, I lift my children to You asking that You would give them a desire to keep themselves pure in body, heart, and mind. Cover them, Lord, with a blanket of spotlessness, guarding them from the habits and mindsets of the world.

Father, I pray You would work Your sanctification in each of my children. Help them avoid any kind of sexual immorality. Teach them to control their minds and bodies in ways that are pleasing in Your sight (1 Thessalonians 4:3-7). Create in them pure hearts and steadfast spirits (Psalm 51:10). Ground them so completely in Your love and wisdom that they have no desire to pursue any relationship or activity that could lead them to harm. Give them the courage to make every effort to be found without blemish, blameless and at peace with You (2 Peter 3:14).

Father, I pray my children would keep their hands clean of working any harm, their hearts purified of any evil ways, and their mouths void of causing pain (Psalm 24:3-4). In Jesus' name, Amen.

33

A PRAYER FOR YOUR CHILD'S FAITH

Father, gift my children with a faith that rests solely on Your great power and not on any wisdom of the world.

Amen.

Habakkuk 2:4
Romans 1:17
1 Corinthians 2:5
Ephesians 1:17-19
Ephesians 2:8-9

Father God, I lift my children to You asking that You give them a desire to love You and seek You with all their hearts. By Your grace, grow in them a foundation that rests solely on Your great power and not on any wisdom of the world. I pray my children will be marked by righteousness, living by faith in all they do (Romans 1:17). Help them trust You more and more each day. Prove Your faithfulness to them in every step, season, and situation in their lives.

Father, incline my children to be well guarded, grounded in their faith, strong and courageous, doing everything in love (1 Corinthians 16:13-14). I pray, Lord, that You would give them the spirit of wisdom and revelation so they may come to know You better. May the eyes of their hearts be enlightened to the glorious inheritance You have in store for those who believe (Ephesians 1:17-19). May their faith be broadened and unbridled, deepened immeasurably, and heightened insurmountably as You display Your great power in their lives. In Jesus' name, Amen.

A PRAYER FOR YOUR CHILD TO LEARN HOW TO FORGIVE

Father, help my children bear with others in love and patience, forgiving as Jesus exemplifies to us.

Amen.

Proverbs 20:22
Matthew 6:14-15
Luke 6:35-36
Ephesians 4:32

Father God, I praise You for Your great and mighty name. I praise you for Your mercy toward us and the complete forgiveness You offer us. You promise that when we confess and repent of our sins, You will remove them from us as far as the east is from the west and will recall our sins no more (Psalm 103:12).

Father, forgiving others is hard for us humans. I pray You would instill Your gracious ways within my children and teach them how to forgive the way You do, wholly and completely.

I pray You would increase love and gentleness in my children so that they may be able to forgive freely and repeatedly. Do not let bitterness, anger, or revenge take root in their hearts. Instead, remind them to bring their troubles, sorrows, and injustices to You. Give them the courage to lay it all at Your feet and then if they need to, lay at Your feet themselves for You to hold and strengthen.

Father, pour our Your great wisdom and grace over my children, equipping them to live out a supernatural ability to forgive. Help them say, "I will not repay or get revenge. Instead, I will wait for the Lord. He will deliver me and avenge me in the appropriate way and in His time" (paraphrased from Proverbs 20:22). Help my children live as peaceably as possible with all people, bearing with others in love and patience, forgiving as Jesus exemplified to us. In Jesus name, Amen.

A PRAYER FOR YOUR CHILD'S EMOTIONS

Father, help my children express and process their emotions in healthy ways.

Amen.

Psalm 12:5-6
Psalm 30:1-3
Psalm 31:9-10, 14-15
Psalm 37:8
Isaiah 61:3

Father, I lift my children to You asking that You inhabit their emotions. Surround them with Your love so they may be encouraged and strengthened to manage and express their feelings in healthy ways. Do not let them be controlled by fits of rage, revenge, jealousy, or malicious words and actions. Instead, give them wisdom and understanding, inclining them toward a gentle and thoughtful spirit.

Father, when my children are overwhelmed, anxious, grief stricken, weary, or troubled in any way, do not let them fall into negative emotional behaviors such as depression, indifference, fear, or hopelessness. Guard them against any detrimental thought processes that could become a stronghold in their lives. When they are frustrated, soothe their souls with Your understanding. When they are distraught, teach them of Your peace. Should they experience sorrow, impress upon them Your unfailing love. Help them trust You in all circumstances so they may live from a heart that is filled with praise and thanksgiving.

Lord, I pray You would bestow on my children a crown of beauty instead of ashes. Anoint them with Your oil of gladness in the midst of mourning. And clothe them in garments of praise so they may be guarded against falling into despair (Isaiah 61:3). Renew my children's hearts and minds, and empower them to overcome any negative emotional behaviors. In Jesus' name, Amen.

36

A PRAYER FOR YOUR CHILD'S EDUCATION

Father, in all of life's schools, may my children come to the conclusion that fearing You and keeping Your commandments is the ultimate duty of their lives.

Amen.

Proverbs 2:1-11
Proverbs 15:33
Proverbs 16:16
1 Timothy 4:7-8
Ecclesiastes 12:13

Lord, bless my children's academic skills and efforts. I pray You would give each of them the desire to learn and ability to increase in knowledge. Help them excel in their strengths while persevering in their weaknesses. Do not let them become discouraged when they cannot grasp things with ease. Instead, may they appreciate and store up the knowledge and experience they gain.

Father, as much as I want my children to flourish in their educations, so much more do I want them to gain wisdom. Your Word teaches us that wisdom preserves the life of its possessor (Ecclesiastes 7:12), that wisdom is supreme (Proverbs 4:7) and the one who gets it will have great insight, able to understand what is right and just and fair. May wisdom enter into their hearts and may knowledge be pleasant to their souls. May discretion protect them and understanding guard them (Proverbs 2:9-11).

Father, I pray that in all of life's schools, may my children come to the conclusion that fearing You and keeping Your commandments is the ultimate duty of their lives (Ecclesiastes 12:13). Keep them grounded, centered on You, broadening their knowledge while maintaining their integrity. In Jesus' name, Amen.

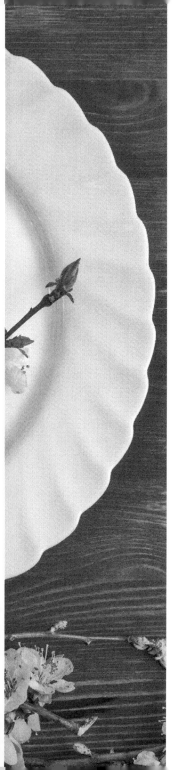

A PRAYER FOR YOUR CHILD'S CALLINGS

Father, help my children walk confidently in the callings You have placed upon their lives.

Amen.

Romans 8:6

Proverbs 3:25-26
Psalm 55:22
Psalm 29:11
Isaiah 32:17
Hebrews 10:35-36

Father God, thank you for these children you have blessed me with. I pray they would come to see themselves as You see them – beautiful, complete, whole, and dearly loved. Lord, give them the courage they need to go throughout their day. Help them walk boldly in Your love. And may they feel Your strength surrounding them even now, enabling them to walk with confidence and assurance.

Lord, give my children quieted hearts. May they be convinced of how deep and wide, strong and endless Your love is for them (Romans 8:37-39), so that when You call my children to do something, they will not doubt or be dismayed. Give them the peace that only comes when we know that we are in Your will (Isaiah 32:17).

Lord, where there is even a shadow of trepidation in my children, remove it from them quickly. Do not let them fear. Be their confidence and do not let them become ensnared by the enemy's plans to swarm them with anxiety. I stand in the gap, Lord, asking that You hold back the flood of insecurities that threaten my children's hearts, minds, and souls.

Lord, help my children see their specific value, worth, and influence. You have made them in Your image, Lord, and in You they are powerful and sure-footed. Enable them to go the heights You have ordained for them. Help them hold on to the hope You have called them to, so that they may be richly rewarded when they have persevered in Your will (Hebrews 10:35).

Father, I pray everything my children do will be pleasing in Your sight, that their efforts may be multiplied, and every step they take may be right and blessed. In Jesus name, Amen.

A PRAYER FOR YOUR CHILD'S WORK ETHIC

Father, make my children strong and courageous, willing to do the work You have called them to.

Amen.

2 Chronicles 15:7
Proverbs 16:3
1 Corinthians 15:58
1 Thessalonians 4:11-12

Father, I lift my children to You, thankful that You have gifted each of them in unique ways. Help them appreciate their talents and flourish in their abilities, so they may be blessed by being a blessing.

Father, regarding the work You have laid out for each of my children, make them strong and courageous, willing to do what You have called them to. When they battle uncertainty or fear, remind them that You are always with them and will never leave them (1 Chronicles 28:20). Help them feel Your presence and Your peace when they face an intimidating task.

Lord, I pray that You would instill perseverance in my children. Help them not give up in doing good, knowing that anything done under Your direction will always be rewarded abundantly (2 Chronicles 15:7). Grow in my children the moral code of steadfastness, keeping them loyal, committed, and focused on Your will for each day of their lives.

Father, I pray now that my children would make it their ambition to lead a quieted life; one that is centered on You and not easily distracted from their heavenly goal. Help them remain content in the plans and places You have for them. May they learn to mind their own business and be diligent in their work, keeping their daily life respectful and respectable, always honoring You and those around them (1 Thessalonians 4:11-12). In Jesus' name, Amen.

A PRAYER FOR YOUR CHILD TO WALK IN VICTORY

Father, cover my children in Your shadow, guarding them from the traps and snares of the enemy. Do not let them become mastered by or enslaved to anything in this world.

Amen.

Psalm 19:13
1 Corinthians 15:57
2 Corinthians 2:14
Galatians 5:1
2 Peter 2:19

Father, I thank You that You have given my children the ability to choose right over wrong, and that You supply the strength and integrity needed to overcome anything that may hinder Your blessings and favor.

Lord, I pray that You would continually lead my children into victory. Do not let them become mastered by or enslaved to anything in this world. Cover them in Your shadow, guarding them from the traps and snares of the enemy. Lord, I stand against any detrimental thought processes, fleshly desires, cravings, habits, and any other thing that will hinder a life of peace and freedom in You. Help each of my children understand that they are not their own. Remind them that their bodies are temples reserved for Your Holy Spirit (1 Corinthians 6:19-20).

Father, keep my children from participating in willful sins (Psalm 19:13). It is for freedom that Christ has set us free. So help my children stand firm, not letting themselves be burdened or enslaved by any yokes of this world (Galatians 5:1). Instead, empower them to be self-controlled and alert (1 Peter 5:8), always being careful how they live, choosing wisely in every situation (Ephesians 5:15-16).

I thank You, Lord, that You are always with my children. I trust You to lead them in a triumphal procession in Christ, blazing a trail of righteousness and leaving behind the fragrance of Your love and grace through them (2 Corinthians 2:14). In Jesus' name, Amen.

A PRAYER FOR YOUR CHILD'S FUTURE

Father, give each of my children a clear vision of what Your best plan is for them, then supply them with the strength to walk according to Your will.

Amen.

Psalm 16:8
Psalm 25:4-5
Psalm 27:4
Jeremiah 42:6
Philippians 3:13-15

Father God, thank You for these children You have entrusted to my care. I pray You would fill in the gaps where my parenting is lacking, so that they will not grow discouraged or their hope dimmed. I lift them to You and ask that You be their comfort and their guide.

Father, when I think of my children's futures I ask that You would give each of them a clear vision of what Your best plan is for them. Then give them the courage and strength to walk in that plan and not go their own ways. May they seek You first in all they do, setting You as their compass and counsel. Show them Your ways, teach them Your paths, guide them in Your truth, and be their hope all their days (Psalm 25:4-5).

Father, I pray my children would be over-comers, able to forget what is behind and press on toward the goal of their prize in Christ Jesus (Philippians 3:13-14). Do not let the enemy hinder them in doing good. I pray my children would stand in faith, resolved to do Your will whether it is favorable or unfavorable to them (Jeremiah 42:6). May they be like oaks of righteousness, a planting of the Lord for the display of His splendor (Isaiah 61:3).

One thing I ask Lord, is that You give my children a desire to seek You with all their hearts, souls, and minds, so they may dwell in Your house all the days of their lives (Psalm 27:4). In Jesus' precious name, Amen.

DEAR MOM
ON SOCIAL
MEDIA

Today I am exhausted. I've put in countless hours caring for my energetic preschooler. I've coached my daughter through a fierce wall of attitude - and remained calm. I've cooked and cleaned, folded and ironed, swept and dusted, planned and shopped, baked and organized, and all I want to do is find caffeine and a brain drain. So I pick up my phone and it's Pinterest and coffee to the rescue.

Five minutes go by. My son asks me to read him a story. "Not now," I mutter, never looking up from the screen to see his sweet inquiring face.

Twenty minutes go by. My daughter asks, "Mom?" for the umpteenth time that day. "What now?" I sighed, just a bit irritated. She slumps away with a, "Never mind." I didn't pursue. Just one more scroll...

An hour later, I'm still there. Head down, blocking out my household. Suddenly, my three year old is bouncing around me hollering, "MOM! I'm hungry!" I glance at the clock and realize dinner will be late if I don't start it now.

In my frustrated rush to get dinner on the table I bark out orders, fully expecting that the same children I so easily ignored a minute ago, should now be pleased to pick up their toys or help set the table. They don't understand why I'm so stressed. They just know they'd better oblige.

After the family is fed, the dishes are done, and the floors are swept, I take another stroll through social media. My daughter, seeing me more engaged in the screen than her presence, quietly slips off to her room and falls asleep without a goodnight.

My son curls up on the end of the couch, knowing I won't have time for a story. He keeps looking at me from time to time, hoping to catch my eye. Eventually, he falls asleep and an hour later I notice the silence. I feel a nudge of guilt as I carry him to bed, yet it's soon forgotten as I scroll through Facebook one more time.

Dear mom, I don't know if you see yourself in this scenario, but we need to wake up. I know you're tired. We all are. I know you need a break. I lock myself in the bathroom to cry and eat chocolate some days.

However, we've got one shot at this raising kids business.

One.

Is social media, your book, or your work really worth blowing it with your children? They need your eyes to notice them. They need your face to light up at their sight. They need your lap to be warmed by. They need your listening ear. Though their concerns may seem small today, what if their struggle is much larger one day? Will they feel safe enough with you to share the tough and scary things of life?

They need your hands to stroke their cheeks. They need your gentleness to remind them that not all of life is hard. They need your example to teach them kindness, love, thoughtfulness, and acceptance. Is that what they are receiving from you?

Instead of reverting to a screen or the work that is calling, curl up with your child for another book. Fall asleep together – one day they'll be too big to snuggle with. Hold your daughter's hand and remember your insecurities at her age. Listen to her. Cry with her. Love her through that tough thing.

Pour into your children just a few minutes longer. Your rest is coming, after bedtime prayers. Or maybe after the fifth goodnight hug and the third time you chase the shadows away, but it's coming.

Mommy dear, you won't remember your best meander through social media. But they will - they'll remember your eyes were glued to the screen when they needed you most. Why not put in a little extra effort and show them how to live life with the ones who matter most.

I promise your rest and quiet is coming. Only it's coming sooner than you'll wish it did.

Courage
Scripture Readings

Isaiah 25:1-9

Isaiah 30:15-18

Psalm 139:1-10

Psalm 139:11-24

Psalm 140:6-13

John 14:23-27

1 Peter 5:2-11

Ephesians 6:10-18

Philippians 1:19-30

Psalm 112:1-9

DEAR DAD ON THE COUCH

get it. Your day was busy. You had many things to do. It feels good to sit down a bit and let the TV think for you. Your wife brings you a cold drink and you relish the feeling of being cared for.

Then your child bounces in. He has a ball and wants you to come outside to play. You say, "No, I'm too tired." Your eyes glued to the screen. He walks away, dejected. Another child is singing to herself while coloring in the chair beside you. You say, "Quiet, I can't hear my TV." She curls up in silence no longer finding joy in coloring a picture for you.

Still another leaps in front of you striking a pose in his superhero cape. You frown and growl, "Move, I can't see my TV." You didn't know he had worked all day, hand sewing his cape and constructing his cardboard and duct tape sword with ultimate care. He walks away with head hanging and shoulders sagging, saddened that his own hero seemed displeased.

Dad, I know you're tired, but you won't remember your best day of TV. Your kids will, though.

They'll remember seeing your disapproving face that favored the view of the screen. They'll remember hearing your rude impatience. They'll remember Daddy had no time and found them to be an inconvenience.

Dad, I know you're tired. You'll get a chance to rest without interruption after you've poured into their lives more than just providing food and a home. They need your voice to cheer them on. They need your deep rumble as you pray over them and to feel your whiskers as you kiss them goodnight. They need your strong arm steadying them as they teeter on their bikes.

They need to see you smile and nod, listening intently while they describe their latest adventure. They need your shoulder to cry on when life is too much and a little pep talk to help them stand for what they believe in.

Daddy, you're their hero.

Their comforter. Their guide. Their encourager. Their safe place. Their strong hand. Their defender.

Their dad. And they need you to stay in that high position.

So when you come home tonight, remember as you drive in the lane, your real job has just begun. One day you won't have this job anymore. And you'll look around in the silence and wonder where they've gone.

10 Psalms for Godly Character

LOVE
Psalm 86:1-17

JOY
Psalm 16:1-11

PEACE
Psalm 23:1-6

PATIENCE
Psalm 62:1-12

KINDNESS
Psalm 116:1-19

GOODNESS
Psalm 18:1-36

FAITHFULNESS
Psalm 143:1-12

SELF-CONTROL
Psalm 37:1-11

WISDOM
Psalm 1:1-6

HUMILITY
Psalm 51:1-19

More from Kaylene Yoder

40 Scripture-Based Prayers
to Pray Over Your Wife

40 Scripture-Based Prayers
to Pray Over Your Husband

A Wife's 40-Day Fasting & Prayer Journal
(devotional)

ABC Scripture Cards
for the Christian Marriage

Prayer Cards for
Husbands, Wives, and Parents

Prayer Challenges

R.E.S.T. Bible Study Method and Journals

and free printable resources can be found at:

https://kayleneyoder.com

Made in the USA
Coppell, TX
22 August 2024

36351962R00057